THE POWER WITHIN US

THE POWER WITHIN US

A LETTER TO AWAKEN SOULS

A CATALYST FOR YOUR KUNDALINI ACTIVATION

DEVIN BROWNE

atmosphere press

TABLE OF CONTENTS

- Letter To Awaken Souls
  3

- Chapter 1 An Introduction—Who Are You?
  5

- Chapter 2 Finding My Spiritual Truth
  8

- Chapter 3 Owning Our Stories
  24

- Chapter 4 Finding Balance
  31

- Chapter 5 Dark Nights and Kundalini Awakenings
  37

- Chapter 6 Releasing the Labels
  45

- Chapter 7 Waking Up
  50

- Chapter 8 Letting Go and Ego Death
  53

- Chapter 9 Steps to Finding Your Truth

56

- Chapter 10 Accepting Your Truth:

A Channeled Message from the Guides

61

- Chapter 11 Kundalani Rising

74

Letter to Awaken Souls

Read this book with an open heart and open mind. Take what is meant for you and leave the rest behind. While I won't pretend to have all the answers, the answers that I do have are meant for those who find this book, pick it up, and begin to read. Enjoy the journey and have fun with it. If, at any point in time, you feel triggered, upset, overwhelmed, or have no idea where to start, I encourage you to find a mental health professional that you connect with that will help you break past your own conditioning patterns that are keeping you stuck in the dark.

This book will press the envelope to metaphysical, religious conditioning, spirituality, paranormal, and so much more. Overall, it will challenge you to open your mind to the truth as you know it to be. I ask that you keep an open mind as you read, and in doing so, you will witness your own inner soul come to life. If you read with different beliefs, engaging with the mindset already closed off to the possibility that there is any truth in this book, then that is okay, too. But may you feel the love I pour into these pages wrapping its arms around you.

This book is designed to awaken your spiritual gifts, trigger your past life memories, and ignite your Kundalini Awakening.

Whether you believe in such things or believe in a higher power or not, I believe you can learn something from this book. Some believe this higher power to be Mother Earth, the universe, Source, Creator, God, Crone, and other names. The truth is he, and I use this term loosely; is known by many names. I believe a memory of who we were before stirs deep inside of every single one of us. If you are picking up this book, there is a reason for it. You were led here. The call to wake up to who you really are is coming. As I said before, enjoy the journey and let what is meant to come for you come. Surrender the outcome.

I have learned that truth changes as you grow and heal. That something that once held true for you at one moment may change and no longer hold true once more information is given, different experiences are lived, and different perceptions are held. It is important that you let go of the rigidity of black-and-white thinking that comes with believing there is only one truth. For there exist many truths, many realities, many experiences, yet we all will perceive them from our own senses on where we are in the journey.

You will find as you read this book that sometimes things are said in a bit of a different way; that is because I am allowing my highest self, the one not on this plane but in the 9D and above, to write through me, I will be channeling some other beautiful beings and spirits to help you along your journey as well. The key is to go with the flow. Let what is meant to come to the surface come. Let your ego not get in the way, for it fears change. Let your highest self come to complete the contracts that you agreed to long ago.

CHAPTER 1

AN INTRODUCTION—WHO ARE YOU?

Who am I?

Well, some would describe me as a mom. Others as a business owner, a friend, a lover, a fighter. There is a list that goes on and on. I'm known by many different names. But let us be honest: we all are. I have learned in the last several years of my own deep mental, spiritual, and physical healing that it doesn't matter the name I am called by anyone else. What matters is the name that I call myself. What matters is how I know myself.

We are told how we should see the world from the moment we are born through external circumstances that are out of our control. Time after time, human conditioning has brought us away from knowing who we once were. From embracing ourselves in the fullness of who we were created to be. In the magic of what we can do.

As living miracles, we breathe, bleed, feel, and heal. Yet, we are conditioned to hate our bodies, ignore our souls, and not trust our minds. We look for external validation and labels to teach us who we are. We look for anything that will help us forget who we have been told we are that, deep down, doesn't line up within our souls.

In my energy practice (Reiki Master, Channeler, 9D Energetic Healer, Akashic Record Reader, Time Traveler), I have relived traumatic events with clients as early as birth. These clients had memories and trauma stored in their bodies as early as coming out of the womb and being forced into a traumatic experience they had no control over. I've walked with clients through their past-life experiences with energy footholds, spiritual hijackers, and more that try to hold onto generational curses or circumstances that no longer serve in this lifetime.

There are many people who will always try to tell you who you are. They will try to tell you who you can be. What you can believe. What is right or wrong. You will feel pushed and pulled by the waves of the world unless you allow yourself to silence the noise. To silence the inner workings of who or what everyone else tells you that you have to be.

Every day, as a child, we do not get to control what happens to us, who our family is, or what is expected of us. As a mom, I can say from experience that I think every single parent eventually looks back and realizes, "Well, crap. I think they'll tell their therapist about that one day." It isn't about being perfect. But it is about being perfectly you. About being who you know yourself to be.

But how do we know ourselves? How do we know who we are? Where are we going? Where do we want to be? We know by allowing the preconditioned patterns to fall away. We know ourselves by doing the work required to heal from those things that trigger us. We know ourselves by recognizing we have needs and not being afraid to ask for those needs to be met. With that, we recognize that we honor ourselves by walking away from situations, circumstances, relationships, beliefs, etc., that no longer serve us. We no longer settle for the narrative of: Oh, that's just how they are, you are being too sensitive, or we have to "forgive" and let go. We learn to become true to ourselves. As we do this, the true essence of who you were before you came into this body is able to come forth. It is able to move forward in full belief and wonder that you are a child of the universe, Creator, and so much more. We do this by listening to the still, small voice that speaks to us: *You are different. You are here for a greater purpose. There is more to life than this.*

Your story is your own. Others, even those involved, while a part of the same story, are simply characters in yours. They have their own book. We see the world through the lens of conditioning, trauma, understanding, cognitive maturity, and much more.

How did I come to know myself? I will be sharing that journey here, along with other tools I have found along the way. My goal with this writing is not to treat, diagnose, or even convince others of their own story or truth. In fact, I will go so far as to say I highly suggest everyone get their own open-minded licensed professional or spiritual coach to talk over things that might come up in their own life/memories as we spend time together. If you don't know where to look, I have a team of them ready to help you, but we will get to that.

But overall, I hope to inspire. I hope to remind you that you are enough. To help you learn to silence the noise and embrace yourself as who you truly are. The authentically beautiful spiritual being that you are. The part of you that is more than human.

CHAPTER 2

FINDING MY SPIRITUAL TRUTH

I remember it like it was yesterday. We gathered around like bees in a hive to watch it transpire. He hadn't shared details with us. Not much, at least. We knew a new experiment was about to begin. One where we could immerse ourselves deeply, learning to be better. To experience this thing called emotions in all forms in one single sitting.

"Let there be light." Blinding, searing brightness shone everywhere as star after star burst forth. Only it wasn't what we would see now. It was like a black hole going backward. As if you pressed rewind on a tape and let it play. Light after light began to appear in the nothingness below us. Galaxies are what they are called now. I watched as a ball of rock took shape, forming with it mountains, valleys, trees, and so much more. It was too beautiful to look away.

I began to shake at the sheer magnitude of energy and power that radiated from Him. It was easy to forget sometimes just how powerful He is. Water began to form, and plants began to grow, creating a living ecosystem. Similar to other worlds that He built, only this time, more magnificently. Everything was connected. Everything had a soul, had life, from the plants and creatures to the sky and sea. There was no such thing as a mundane creation. Everything served a purpose. I watched as the grass began to grow, coming with it all sorts of magnificent flowers, trees, and shrubs. How had He thought of all of this? The amount of time to come up with these ideas alone is incredible. But I guess time doesn't matter when you're a deity.

Creatures as tall as buildings began to walk this new rock formation. I watched as, with a twist of His fingers, working within our energy network and in detail, He formed all the animals. "Someone's had a little too much time on his hands," I hear spoken behind me. I didn't turn to look at who said it. This was too magnificent to even turn my eyes away for a second. I had to watch. I had done my own creating of worlds before, but this was on a whole new level. It hit me as I began to see the inner echo system of each living creature—He created them like us. They could heal themselves. They could regenerate. Their bodies each left with their own energy pool. How was He doing this? How was He leaving a little piece of himself inside of each of them yet still remaining whole himself? It was remarkable. I couldn't wait to go there. To see it up close and personal. To immerse myself in the feelings.

I watched as he began to create a being that looked remarkably like us. The Source energy network mirroring my own inner power and magic. Its body looking similar to my angelic presence, only it was contained. The energy was still limitless, only shelled off from each other. Yet, all was still connected. I watched as each well was locked into a vortex of seven major wells running down the body. It gave them life beyond just flesh. They could access deep into the Source by breaking through each of those shells and anchoring into the Earth, then onto other dimensions. "How incredible," I said to my counterpart standing next to me. "I can't wait to go there."

What you read above is my detailed memory of creation I had put into a book many years ago; I was going to write my memories as a novel. I wanted to speak my truth. I needed to embrace it and share it, but the only way I could think of doing so in a "safe" or acceptable manner was if I put it in the form of something that seemed very close to fiction. I could never get past this part of the chapter. I couldn't take something so beautiful as the memory above and laden it with stories I know to be true yet label it as fiction. My truth changes the deeper I go. My understanding lengthens as memories continue to return.

GETTING PERSONAL

In this chapter and the next, I will get personal with some of my own story. My own truth, which every year changes, evolves, and adapts as more memories, information, and inner wisdom come forth. It comes forth because I am at a place of inner safety to allow it to do so. Then, I will teach you how you can discover for yourself who you are. I will share with you how I began embracing who I was and what I could do. How I brought my magic and that of others back into being. Some of us are afraid to own our identities, beliefs, or interests, and some of us aren't yet awake enough to see what it is. But it doesn't change who you are at the deep core energetic level. Some of you are angels, fairies, dragons, and sleeping beings of old. I see you. You vibrate at a different level; your souls call out and visit me in the astral. But this perpetual wakened slumber stems from past life traumas, engrained fear from witch hunts, fear of breaking out of the matrix, but mostly current societal, familial, and religious conditioning. We have been in a dark spiritual age for the last three thousand-plus or so years, keeping us from seeing so clearly what is right in front of our faces.

Some of you are just on the cusp of waking up and discovering who you are. This chapter shares how I embraced myself and my spiritual truth. How I decided to live as someone fully awake versus hiding like a candle under the bed. May it be the seed that takes root in your own mind, bringing with it life and your own truth.

So, who do I say that I am? I am an angel, starseed, light-worker, Kundalini activator, spiritual guide, and leader. I am a daughter of the goddess you once knew as Isis and engrained as one with the Star Mothers of old. You may have forgotten who they are after so many years. I am a being of light, come into the body of a human. A spiritual being here for a human existence. Not a human being here for a spiritual experience. Many of you who have picked up this book are the same. You are not merely "human." It is one of the reasons this title spoke to you, and you must read on. I am a Kundalini Activator. I am here to bring you back "online" to remember yourself and who you once were and still are. I am a teacher and guide. I am a being who chooses to operate out of unconditional love, even to those whom others would deem unworthy. I am one who works with spirits, ghosts, fae, dragons, Gaia, and her children. I was sent to wake up you sleeping souls that have forgotten who you are, and to usher back in with my other awakened brothers and sisters, an ascension like never before.

If at any point reading the above you became emotional, something stirred inside of you, then you too are what I am lovingly calling a Kundalani. A spiritual being that decided to come down, break the trauma bonds of generations, the religious conditionings of old, the hatred that disguises itself as love and servitude. You came to alter the planet's vibration simply by existing at this very moment on the ground in which you stand. Let that sink in right now: YOU are that powerful. You are here to usher in a new vibration to the planet. And it is time to wake up my beautiful souls.

Looking back at history, many of us came time and again and were known by other names: Ishtar, Isis, Athena, Thoth, Thanos, Aphrodite, Zeus, Dionysus, Hermes, Apollo, Poseidon, Ares, Prometheus, Condor, Thor, Jupiter, Medusa, the Monarch

Being, and more. Gods and Goddesses. By embracing and using powers that have long been thought dead and turned into stories, we walked the earth with you once very openly. Yet we are here and very much alive. Only until recently, the vibrations of the Earth were not at a place to allow us to speak so openly with you again. We are all one with the Source, the Creator, the energy that beats with life, and in being so, we are all indeed the Source. We simultaneously exist on this plane and in others, sometimes in multiple carnations at the same time. This is many of you, and it is time to open your eyes to see. Some of these deities were and still work as the fallen angels going against the Source, set on destruction, mayhem, and keeping us in the dark. Their power is strongest when feeding off your anxiety, fears, and conditioning. Some of you already want to put this book down out of the conditioned fear of sin, damnation, or overall discomfort of a soul purpose spoken that rubs against your conditioned ego.

For most of you who are already balking at this idea, you are mostly likely coming from a religious, and conditioned perspective, and I want you to stop and think: Does it not say in your Bible that angels saw that humankind was beautiful and wanted to procreate with them? So, they came down in human form and had babies; thus, the giants were formed. Does it not say that Moses threw a staff on the ground, and it became a snake, that he parted the Red Sea, that the language of tongues (which is light language or the language of the stars) was gifted to those who opened themselves back up to their truth? That you could see the tongue of fire above their heads when that gift was granted?

That language of "tongues" that exists in so many Christian communities is our light language. The language of heaven, of Source, of old. It does not only exist in the organized religious community. For those of you from other religions, you seem much more open to the ideas of something different. But most of you in religious cultures are stuck on this perpetual loop that truth is black and white and fits in a box. But we are here. I know many angels and spiritual beings personally, and many are remembering who they are from of old, why they came, and what their soul mission is. It is time to wake up, my sleeping angels, deities, travelers, healers, priests, priestesses, fae, dragons, starseeds, and all other beings of light.

How do I know this? It is a deep inner knowing because of who I am. It is memories of past, present, and future premonitions. It is the answers that exist on the inside of me, just as your own answers exist on the inside of you. Many of us angels of light have come into ourselves in full remembrance in the last five years, but all of us knew since birth that we were different. We vibrate at a different level than most. We can spot each other the moment we see each other. If you are not yet awake, it may seem like a familiarity to someone you haven't seen before. It may seem like they glow in a way. They are full of light, laughter, kindness, and strength.

For myself, my knowing has been an overall lifelong event of hiding, denying, or blending. I always knew that I was different in a way. Since I could write, I filled journals with what I now recognize as "channeled text" from the Creator, Source, and my guides. I would have visions, dreams, or visits from my spirit guides, other angels, ghosts, etc. I can't pinpoint exactly when my gifts were found. In a way, they were always there. But I was taught that my gifts were wrong, and I began to hate myself and forget who I truly was. Throughout my childhood, a lot of what I felt I could do or see wasn't acceptable. I grew up in a very fundamentalist Christian community. I was allowed to say in a Church setting I saw a "demon" or saw a "vision," and it was accepted as truth. I could tell the future premonition I received to someone by saying I had a dream about them last night; goodness, I used that one a lot. But to say that I could look at people and see past their skin, that everyone was not only surrounded and intertwined with vibrant colors, but that I could see deep into their spiritual streams. Into the energetic Source network I remember so vividly, into the very essence of who they were on a soul level. That I could see their past life wells as they formed a deep spiral staircase through their Sacral Chakras. That I could see beings that appeared not to be there to anyone else: ghosts, spirits, angels, dark entities, creatures out of a mythical fairy tale. This was something I didn't even understand how to put words to myself until I was much older.

As a kid, I would walk through a store and see people, hearing words: divorce, drugs, death, cancer, etc. And would know instantly that the person I was looking at was dealing with those things. My entire life, I would be sitting alone in my house and have someone I hadn't heard from in years pop into my head. This was accompanied with a word, or picture of an event, or trauma. I would later get confirmation that what I saw or heard transpired.

Living in the abusive and very religious environment I did as a child, I did not feel safe enough to explore this truth. I didn't feel like I could own it. Even after I learned my real name, the spiritual name given to me before coming to this body, I felt I had to stay hidden.

I didn't feel that I would be accepted or understood. Slowly, over time, I began to deny it was anything other than the acceptable names under Christianity. Most of the time, especially when out in public, I was overwhelmed and would completely block myself off energetically to everything around me: sight and sound. I would open myself up only when I knew it was a need I had to meet in order to keep myself safe. I taught myself to live a dissociated existence. I find it interesting that many Starseeds (earth angels) whom I know and see out in public, or even online all have a very distinct aura, some have auric energetic wings, all glow differently than other entities, and your vibrations to me are as obvious as the sun during the day. Most of you will be waking up from a Christian or organized religious, familial, or cultural conditioning trap. This wasn't an accident; we were trapped on purpose to take away our power. We agreed to certain life experiences to access our Kundalini Activation, and spiritual giftings.

Looking back with the understanding I have now, I recognize that by denying myself spiritually, I was also denying myself physically, mentally, and emotionally to be who I was. I would deny and betray myself to appease anyone who held a place in authority. I do believe, though, that my gifts of intuition were also very much honed by the chaos at home. Lemonade out of lemons.

When channeling, I would ask who I was and why I had my gifts. I would get an answer: an angel, but I still didn't feel like I could accept it. I am reminded time and again of different religious texts by my guides that rang home the truth of this:

Do not forget to show hospitality to strangers, for by so doing, some people have shown hospitality to angels without knowing it. Hebrews 13:2 <u>The Holy Bible</u>

Fatir 35:1 All praise be to Allah, the Fashioner of the heavens and earth, Who appointed angels[1] as His message bearers, having two, three, four wings.[2] He adds to His creation whatever He pleases.[3] Verily Allah has power over everything. <u>The Quran</u>

The Hindu text the Bhagavad Gita speaks of angels as deities that walked among us. (I will get into this a little later as this plays deeply into my own memories and past lives. Myself and other angels I know. We were the embodiment of some of these deities and the names by which we were called.)

Again, this was all unacceptable to believe as a child. And even as an adult, I felt it was wrong or "sinful." It was something that, if I believed or acted on, I thought I would be forever torn away from the love of my Creator into a fiery hell. Again, this is religious fear-induced conditioning. A reason I am highly against organized religions teaching an umbrella of authority or knowledge. All the answers to who you are and what you need exist inside of you. We have just been taught to ignore our souls, don't trust our minds, and hate our bodies: the opposite of what we must do.

I remember when I was 13 years old, I was alone in my bedroom channeling the Creator, universe, Crone, Source, Mother, guides, highest self, etc.—whatever name you want to give your deity of light, I was writing in a journal what was being spoken to me. I came outside to find one of my parents in the kitchen. I was excited to share what I had just been told. That I was chosen to be here. I was chosen to help usher in a new stage for the "angelic" (now recognizing more than just angels) and humanity as one. That I was different and the need to embrace it. As I told my parent that I wanted to share something with them that I felt "God" had spoken to me during prayer, I began with the only acceptable way I could think of to back up my claim. I had been taught not to trust myself but knew that what I heard was truth, so I needed to defend it from the beginning. *You know how it says in the Bible that all are called, but few are chosen? I am chosen. I was chosen to be here right now for this time.* But the response I got even from the start of that story told me that I wasn't safe. That I could not speak my truth. I was told that I couldn't talk like that. That I was no better or different than anyone else in that house and that I was prideful and sinful thinking that. I was shamed for admiring who I was and why I was here. I felt guilty for thinking good things about myself. I felt shamed for even believing I was extraordinary or different. But that is the thing. We all are different. But I am different from other neurotypical humans because I am not "human." But that difference is what makes me special. It is what makes you special. Other angels and spiritual beings that are here are struggling to wake up because they struggle to believe and embrace that they are unordinary, embracing it as extraordinary. That is what we need to change. We are afraid to be misunderstood when being willing to be misunderstood is actually your very greatest superpower.

When I astral projected into the ethers for the first time as a teenager, I never knew how to explain that experience to a religious household. I was in my bedroom meditating and praying, and I was suddenly astral projecting; though my physical body was in my room, my mind was not. My vision became like a movie before my eyes. I was taken to this place deep in nothingness (the ether), and a being appeared before me. His face shone bright like the sun. I could barely look at him. He was full of peace and love. And he gave me a message of who he was and how he would walk with me on this journey. He was one of my guides and one who still guides me today. I ran into my parents' room to try to explain what had just happened, and I began to cry as I was so full of awe and wonder. I was greeted with, "It sounds like what you saw really scared you." I said, "No, it was wonderful." But then it was put to the side as if I had dozed and had a dream that was to be forgotten and to let it go.

I knew that they were wrong. Time and again, something in my soul screamed that this wasn't in alignment. The life I was living wasn't for me. Not because I was any better than anyone else; I am not. But I am different, and so are you.

MY BELIEFS

Before I get too far here, I think a little segue into what I actually believe and know to be the truth *now* is in order. I have seen the Creator of this realm many times. In fact, when I project myself to the Creator's "throne room" and spend time in his presence (again, I use *Him* loosely) I speak to Him face to spiritual face. For days after, I will get comments from strangers on how my skin glows or that something looks different about me from those that know me. I used to just laugh and tell them it's genetic or my plant-based eating. I had never felt that "Oh, I just came from an astral heaven" would be a believable answer. But now I will give the honest answer. It's how it should be. We should be willing to say that I have spent time with Mother Earth and found her truths. That I wrapped myself up in the ethers of heaven and allowed that vibration to bring me home to myself here on earth. All of us awakened beings are created with that pathway to get there, though some of us can get there deeper than others. But all of us spiritual beings: angels, shamans, travelers, healers, high priestesses, fairies, dragons, starseeds, lightworkers, etc. can get there directly.

We are all created, human and spiritual beings alike, to be surrounded daily by the Source with her loving light and energy. A piece of the Source runs through every single one of us. Just like my memory of creation. A living, breathing piece of the Source runs through every single one of us. We are within Source. Source is within us.

WHAT DO I BELIEVE?

I believe organized religion was put here as a method of control. It keeps those gifted like me and others I know in a bubble of fear and self-doubt. I believe there are many of you who are like me. You know you are different, yet you struggle to wake up. You are afraid, or maybe you just don't know the way. You have been living like a candle under the bed, letting your light shine in the darkness but only so much. I believe it is time to step out from the shadows and, like the moon, shine in the full glory of the night. If you are reading this text and this begins to spark emotion, it is you, child, that I speak to. Your ego will try to say, "No, this isn't it." But it is.

I believe every religious text, no matter if it is the Bible, Torah, Quran, Hindu, or Buddhist texts, etc., each holds a portion of the truth. I do not believe one is right above the other.

With that in mind, the belief that I couldn't be open or grow my gift was all based on my own religious conditioning and my own lack of self-love and acceptance. I believe in the gods of old, not in the way that they are, in fact, meant to be worshiped, but that they still live, watch over us, and work with us as guides on our ascension journey into that of our highest self.

There was once a pastor of a Church I was a worship leader for, though still hidden in my own identity, who began praying for the psychics and witches who were coming to the area for a convention. He begged God that they would turn their faith to him and come use their gifts to glory and goodness as prophets instead of witches and fortune tellers. I sat there and thought to myself, but what is the difference? I can do what they do. I actually knew some of the witches and tellers that were going to be at that convention. They were beautiful beings of light. A little segue—Yes, you can pull from the light or the dark energies, and we will get into that later in this book. But what about the label that in certain beliefs or teachings makes something evil or taboo?

I know myself now. I no longer deny who I am or what I can do. I embrace it. I am extraordinary. I know my spiritual name. I know my history. I remember creation being formed. I remember the beauty as the sun and moon were spoken into existence. I know I picked my parents so that I could get to where I am today through generational giftings, but also the lessons I would learn through generational curses and hardships. Some unforeseen free will and all added in that mix. Each one of you was sent here for a purpose; some of you chose your own, others it was requested of. None is too big or too small.

I know my freedom to embrace myself and then explore and push the envelope of normal will help free others stuck in their own conditioning and denial of truth. Sometimes, we just have no idea where to even start. Many times throughout my life, as loud as if you were sitting in front of me, I have heard a clear, audible voice with directions on what I needed to do. I always have premonitions and visions that come true or warn of what could come. Ever since I can remember, I could see things that others couldn't when I opened myself up to allow it.

My earliest memory was when I was about three years old. I was staying at my grandmother's for the night. She had a certain song she would sing to me every night before bed, and for some reason, she shared with me that she was going to sing that song at my wedding one day. I looked at her, and though I couldn't see her future as a vision, I remember I felt it. I knew she wouldn't be there. I said, "Grandma, you can't say that. You won't be there." She argued lovingly and said, "No, baby girl, I promise I will be there." "No, Grandma, you may die in a car crash before that day happens." When I was 16, she passed out at the wheel of her car due to a drop in blood pressure, crashed her car, and passed away.

What I can see isn't always a gift. In fact, I blocked it out for so many years as much as I could because I was over-whelmed. It was scary to accept it when I didn't understand it. I believed that it was evil and wrong and struggled to see how good could happen from it. It was hard to see the light in a world that reeked of evil. But then I realized that it was my perception of the gift that was wrong. It was the label I put on it. Now, I recognize that so much of that was religious condi-tioning. I wasn't safe to share. I had to create a place of safety for myself to grow. I used my channeling as prayer, prophecy, and other spiritual names that were acceptable in the religious setting I grew up in. I believed with my whole heart that this was the only way that I could live. I believed that I was able to make the biggest difference by staying in these rooted struc-tures. It was what we were "called" to do.

But finding and embracing my spiritual truth and beliefs was the first step. But then, I had to be willing to let those beliefs and gifts flow, bend, and change. In doing so, I gave myself permission to ask questions, to find answers. In doing so I found my physical, spiritual, and mental truth. I stopped denying and truly listened to the inner voice inside of myself, I felt safe. I felt loved. I knew what was spoken was truth. I had heard that voice all my life. I knew instinctively what to do in my own worship ceremonies. In my healing practice, my hands would form symbols and movements intuitively, and the client would get the relief they sought. I humbly accepted that I was a walking, breathing, living miracle.

MY KEY TO BREAKING CONDITIONING

What is the key to how I found my truth outside of the conditioning? I began to be okay even if I thought differently than the other people around me. Even if I couldn't tell them. I began to recognize I cared too much about others' perceptions of me. I began to recognize that my worth was in how others perceived me or in how happy they were with my behavior. My worth was rooted in how well others did with my help and not my own accomplishments. And with that truth, I took responsibility for the toxic dynamic I was creating with the codependent choices. I began to exit the rat race, and the expectations of: this is how life is meant to be lived.

Slowly, I found a few friends here or there who believed as I did. I began to be open about what I could see, feel, and what I knew about my past life experiences and why I was here for this one. As I began to open up to accept this truth, I began to gain self-confidence. I began to realize there were people out there who would love me for me, as I was, without having to put myself in a religious box. And as I put myself out there for those friends, more came. It's amazing when you open yourself up to your truth, growth, and ascension how the others aligned on that same path also begin to walk forward to meet you.

As I stated before, I then began to recognize and take responsibility for my own part that I played with where I was in that moment. Embracing my spiritual truth allowed me to embrace who I was as a person. And by embracing who I was as a person, I began to realize that the life I had around me wasn't authentically me. It was a shadow version of what I thought was acceptable. I lived as I felt I was expected to live. I didn't want that for myself anymore. I wanted to embrace my individuality. I wanted to love myself, my beliefs, and use my giftings to change the world by being who I knew I was.

It was time to break the mold. To release my "inner goddess" and let myself be who the Creator made me to be in every single way. To love myself as I did so. And by loving myself, giving myself to face the truth of the life I was surrounded with. Was I happy? Was I safe? Did I feel loved? Did I feel secure? Did I have room to grow in the way that I felt I needed? Then, as I faced the emotions of what I truly felt and what I wanted, I was able to figure out how to create my physical space to be in alignment with who I was and what I wanted. I was able to clearly see what I needed to do for myself.

My needs involved walking away from my marriage that was no longer in alignment with what I needed or what I wanted for myself. My need was walking away from a faith I claimed as my own for 35 years. My need was to dive into other spiritual beliefs, rituals, and unknown knowledge to discover what rang true for me. It seemed to others that I had taken a 360 on my beliefs, but I hadn't. I still worship the same Source and light I did when I was young. Only it has a deeper name and meaning to me now. I am still me: a person full of love, light, kindness, and everything in between. I just am no longer willing to live the muted version of myself with self-hatred, shame, and judgment. I am not willing to let anyone tell me I had to believe a certain way, and only a certain way. In the place I was, I couldn't change and feel emotionally or mentally safe. So, I left and created my own safe space.

As I did this my soul family came in and rallied around me. I wasn't as alone as I feared I would be. I had more family living as my authentic self within my small group than I had with crowds of people living as a muted version of myself.

CHAPTER 3

OWNING OUR STORIES

"Owning our story can be hard, but not nearly as difficult as spending our lives running from it. Embracing our vulnerabilities is risky but not nearly as dangerous as giving up on love and belonging and joy, the experience that makes us the most vulnerable. Only when we are brave enough to explore the darkness will we discover the infinite power of our light."
– Brene Brown

This was one of the hardest truths for me to surrender to. While it makes sense now on the other side of the dark tunnel, it didn't at the beginning of the race line. How would uprooting my life, going against everything I have believed or been taught to follow that nudging of truth that I stuffed and hid in a box deep in the corner of my soul, bring me to a better or brighter place of light? When I decided I had to walk away from my marriage for my own health and the example of my children, I had to face the fact that I wasn't going to lose just what I considered my entire life. I was going to have to say goodbye to my long-term extended family. I was going to lose friendships. I was going to lose the core religious system of support I had built around myself. It was scary to own my truth. To no longer deny what I had been believing, pursuing, or practicing in secret. No longer feeling guilty about wanting to pursue my faith deeper, or to explore other beliefs and truths that held connection deep in my soul. I had to accept that my past had conditioned me in a way to accept less than what I wanted. That abuse had conditioned me to accept less than I deserved. It had taught me that I wasn't good enough ever, and I had to live and find my value in everyone else. That I had to settle. But the biggest part of all of that was: I had to come to the acceptance of the truth that I had been abused and conditioned. Only then could I face the demons that had come my way. When I began my healing journey by adding my therapist, she asked me what I was scared of the most as we delved into my past. I told her honestly that it was how it was going to change my relationships, not just with my spouse but with my family and friends.

I had grown up in the Church and was conditioned to believe that the only way to reach my full potential was to serve others before myself. To speak a certain way, believe a certain way, to act a certain way. While I was always me and still am: kind, loving, optimistic, etc., I had no boundaries and denied myself permission to have an identity outside of how I could help others. Because of this, I would deny my own desires, needs, wants, joys, and even that deep calling that cried out to my soul that I was made for more than this. That I deserved more than this. Over time, I found myself getting depressed. Feeling empty. I was getting angry at being taken for granted. Then, I would reprimand myself for feeling angry. "How dare I?" as I threw myself on the sword of martyrdom: Treat others like you want to be treated. Put others above yourself. I had no understanding of boundaries or how important they were. I was lost in the sea of others while desperately trying to claw my way up for air. I felt responsible for the healing journey and emotions of those around me. But while I focused on them, I lost myself. But the truth is I felt responsible for everyone else's happiness and growth but my own. I was taught this inadvertently as a child.

One of the hardest things I ever had to do was face my past. It will most likely be one of the hardest things you also have to face. But do not just look at it; stop minimizing how situations affect you because you were told "they were no big deal" or "not that bad." I have found that many of the awakened souls that are waking are arising from very dark areas and pasts. But the reason for this is not an accident. We all need to face our dark night of the soul in order to wake up. To allow our Kundalini Awakening to transpire; more on that later.

We have to face our traumas and conditioning from the very beginning. We have to set the foundation of love and peace for future generations. How did I do this? I started from the beginning. I owned *my* truth, my trauma, but also my responsibility in allowing toxic patterns to continue as I became an adult. I emphasize this is *my* trauma and truth because, as stated above, the others in my story have their own books. They have their own perceptions of the truth. There exist multiple truths in the same reality. I had to accept that. But with that truth, I also had to stop diminishing what my soul went through as a child that affected me into adulthood. Then, for what I was allowing in as an adult, I had to recognize I was now responsible—because I was no longer a child. I had to accept and recognize that my truth had a profound impact on why I was living the life I was. I had to allow healing to come through facing the darkness. I faced my trauma, sadness, self-sabotage, and everything in between. I had to be okay with recognizing, as I speak out on what occurred, what I feel to be the truth, what I know as my own truth, that some will believe me, others will call me crazy, some will be confused, and others judgmental. As my vibration and beliefs began to shift, I had to accept and watch as many friends and some family walked away. Some walked away because we were no longer in alignment with the way we lived our lives, others because it was easier, some out of judgment, some out of confusion, some out of hurt, and some due to lies spoken out about me and my choices. Owning your truth can cause those around you discomfort. I had to be okay with that while also letting myself grieve those losses. Then, there were some relationships; while not disengaging altogether, they took on a new role. A new pattern.

The healing I embraced went deeper than my divorce and religious conditioning. I had to recognize the toxicity in which I grew up. I had to put a name to the childhood experiences that played a role in me believing I had to hide who I was. I had to name the abuse, toxicity, and trauma I both witnessed and experienced. I had to recognize it for what it was. I gave a name to this trauma, whether it was through friends, family members, religious leaders, etc. I took off the rose-colored glasses and stopped justifying the low vibrational actions or "wrong" behavior of others.

I owned the truth that, as a fully functioning adult, I no longer had to give these things power over me. I gave voice to the truth that it was a choice. With this truth, I was no longer disassociating. I was able to recognize that I was the one responsible for getting my needs met. I was only responsible for my own emotions, not those around me. I was responsible for my own actions, even those that seemed involuntary. I needed to learn to respond versus reacting. I had to accept that I was what you would call codependent, and I had to work tirelessly to break those toxic cycles. I took responsibility for my own part I played in toxic dynamics as an adult. I took ownership of my anxious attachment style, which had me taking everything very personally and would trigger me into a state of emotional insecurity. I had to actively decide to change this. I had to learn to set boundaries and no longer let people use me or my good nature to meet all their needs, making their lives easier, all while ignoring my own self-care. I had to take responsibility for the fact that I let them. I had to own the fact that, as I healed, I myself would become a trigger for other people. As I owned my truth, the truth of who I was as an awakened soul, that I would make others uncomfortable and possibly even trigger them as I began to shine like a mirror, reflecting those things in their lives that they also have stuffed in a box, ignoring in the corner like I had.

I had to learn that self-care is not, when every couple of months and I was on empty, I did something nice for myself. Self-care is a way of life. It's creating a life around yourself that gives you daily peace. Daily joy. It's creating a space for yourself that allows you to have a safe space where you don't have to walk on eggshells. You don't have to hide your beliefs or disagreements about beliefs. It's a place where you are surrounded by people who love and accept you for you. A place where even on your bad days, when your ego seems to get the better of you, you know you are still loved and accepted. Self-care is a lifestyle. A lifestyle where your soul, the very essence of who you were before you came into this body, gets to rule and reign every day versus the ego. I don't think I can possibly stress that enough.

How do we own our truth? For starters, you sit and face it. There are so many of us who never sit still. We constantly go from one distraction to the next. Some of them are productive; others are mindless. I know from my own example: I was one of the most productive disassociated people you could name. I was a super mom, super wife, super business owner, worship leader, caregiver, friend, supporter, foster mother, spiritual guide, you name it. I was always looking for ways to make myself useful to others. I was, in essence, all things to everyone else, but nothing to myself. The first step is recognizing how you really feel about where your life is. Without judgment, just being truthful. This is where an open-minded therapist will come in handy. Sometimes friends can be this too, but I found we don't always feel safe enough to tell our friends the truth about what is going on in our heads or behind closed doors. I never did. I had been conditioned to never say "no" and to never feel angry, so I felt too guilty for feeling anger or negative emotions and was convinced something was wrong with me.

Grab a pen and paper: Sit with yourself and truly look at how you feel about your life at this moment—without judgment. How do you feel about your current truth? What are you happy with? What are you not happy with? From that list, you can decide if it is something you can change or not or if you want to.

Owning the truth of where we are, where we came from, and where we want to be doesn't mean that you go out and share everything with everyone. It doesn't mean that you shout all your trauma, healing, or identity from the rooftops—though if you feel that would help, you do have every right to tell your story in whatever way will bring healing to you. It is your truth. But it is about why. Why is this affecting me, why do I want to share, and where is this going to take me? Do I want to give a certain emotion or event this much power? We also must recognize how our past conditioning, beliefs, etc., are affecting what we perceive as our truth.

I highly recommend the book *How to Do the Work* by Dr. Nicole Lepera if you feel like you need to face your inner conditioning and self-truth but have no idea how or where to start.

I have found that the only way forward is backward. It's going to the beginning of where your beliefs are that may be limiting you. It's going to where everything is rooted. It's going back to where you were so you can get to where you want to go. It's facing the memories of trauma not only in this life but in your past lives, too.

As you own your truth, even those behaviors you are ashamed of, or maybe choices you made that you wish would have been different, remember to show yourself love, grace, and kindness. We all do the best we can with the level of emotional maturity and cognitive understanding that we have.

As you move past where you are now into where you want to be, you can remember that and let go of the power that other's treatment of you has. This is not to say you do not have boundaries or do not make people take accountability for their behavior toward you. But it is recognizing the truth that the only person you can control as you awaken is yourself.

CHAPTER 4

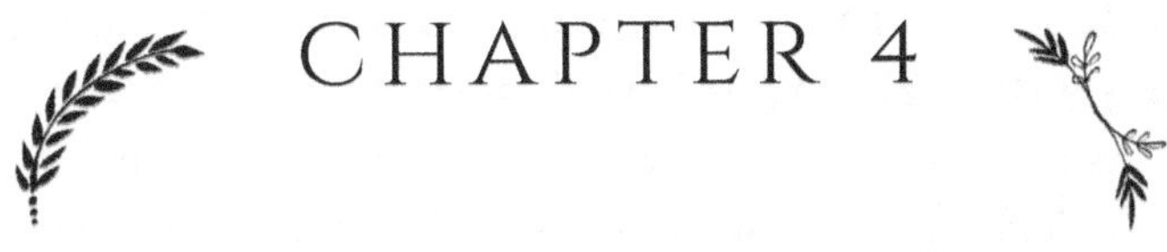

FINDING BALANCE

Newton's Third Law states that for every action or force in nature, there is an equal and opposite reaction. I have found this to be true in more than just nature. We can find this to be true in the spiritual, religious, and political realms as well.

Likewise, there are the yin and yang energies inside of each of us. The balance between the feminine and masculine energies. There exists a fight between the ego (divine masculine) and the soul (divine feminine). There exists a fight between the past and the present. I will not sit here and pretend to have all the answers. In fact, as I learn more, grow more, and even experiment more in my own practices and rituals, I find the truth is never black and white, but there is balance everywhere if you let it come. Your truth can change and shift. I think it is important to note that you must allow that. Think of it in the way an optical illusion is put together; when you first look at it, it looks like a picture of two vases, but then, as you move over and look from a different perspective, it turns into two heads facing each other. Our truth grows and changes in much the same way. You look at your truth from the viewpoint you are currently observing from (the stage of healing you are in), and as you move to another position, the picture changes (entering a new stage of healing). In both stages, the image you saw was a hundred percent there and a hundred percent correct for you at that moment. But the truth is so much deeper than it seems at any given moment.

While I hope to encourage others to awaken and know themselves on their own spiritual journeys, the only way I can do that is by sharing what I do know as of this moment to be my truth. The truth of what I remember, what I am remembering as I accept and love myself, what my deep inner knowing says is true, and what I have experienced. I can tell you how I broke through my matrix. How I let go of the lies that held me back and away from the knowledge contained deep within me. How I faced what, to me, felt like the scariest thing I ever had to do: Walking away from the beliefs I had known to be "true" for so long to embrace what my soul, heart, and mind screamed over and over again was true. Letting go of the idea that I needed to be understood. That I needed to follow the pattern of x, y, and z. Letting go of relationships that were no longer in alignment with where I was. Finding balance.

One thing we have forgotten over time is how to let our souls live for us. How to live in the moment. How to dwell in the spirit. We don't have the conditions here on our Earth planet anymore that would allow us to come into our humanity from a safe space and keep it as we grow. We are stuck in this perpetual war of opposite reactions. It's a place where individual ritual and spiritual expression would have us embrace who we are now, who we once were, and get us back to our roots, yet too many organized religions feed on power and control and would have us press forward in bondage, forgetting who we were, and banning all things that threaten that thought pattern of black and white thinking as evil.

One of my own struggles that I had to break away from was the imbalance of my yin and yang. On a physical level, I was goal-oriented, focused, and constantly hunting or searching for the next project. I was fully in my masculine survival energy. This imbalance made it so that I couldn't even rejoice in my current successes. My need for control to feel safe or to feel valued was destroying me little by little. I never felt like I was enough. I never knew how to rejoice in the moment. I set a goal, and I WOULD get it. I am one of those inspiring people who, if I set a goal, there is nothing stopping me from achieving it. There is no such thing as "I can't" in my vocabulary. I can and will change my mind on if I want something or not, but if I truly want it, I will manifest it in my life. But the endless need to force things, to run out of fear, fight out of fear, or the imbalance between masculine confidence and feminine play was missing. Occasionally, I would find that balance. If I'm being truthful, some of my best and most amazing memories are when I was able to manifest things into my life that I truly had no idea how it was going to happen. I simply set the intention and desire out to the universe, then sat back and let it work. I witnessed miracles in action.

We as humans have this annoying tendency where we want to control everything. To have an answer for everything. This goes for the scientific and spiritual. We need to be right. But why? Why would it hurt us to open our eyes to the *truths of others* around us? It doesn't mean you need to take on their beliefs. It doesn't mean you need to take on their practices. But what a difference this world would make if we were goal-oriented in a way that allowed us to relinquish control and let the Creator guide us undeniably in the direction we are meant to be heading.

I began to find my balance between my yin and yang when I embraced my spiritual side without hiding it from those surrounding me. It came when I began to be open about my daily practice. I found my balance when I faced my physical and mental trauma, giving myself permission to exit survival mode. I found my balance when I accepted the truth of how I really felt about the relationships I allowed around me. Balance came when I looked at the truth that the life I was living was not one that left me feeling balanced. I was honest with myself that I was exhausted and burnt out. I was a hamster on the run of a never-ending wheel. I began shifting back into balance when I began to accept that I was okay with believing differently. I began to step into my divine feminine, my soul journey and remembrance, as I found freedom in believing what was close to my heart. I was okay embracing the paranormal giftings that I have without shame. When I decided to embrace what the Creator had spoken to me over and over again about who I was.

The catalyst for my own kundalini activation was when I owned up to my truth that I was living a muddled life. I was living one that did not feel like it fulfilled me, with the beliefs that had been engrained and conditioned in me for 30+ years. I realized I had adjusted myself to the lies that I had to live under these rules, these guidelines, and consigned myself to the idea that the truth, my salvation, was this way and only this way. I gave witness to my truth that I was out of balance. My activation began when I faced myself in all the real rawness of how I really felt, without judgment or shame, and let myself feel it, acknowledge it, and grieve it. It was then that I realized I no longer wanted to live a disassociated life. I no longer wanted to live a life where I was shutting off my emotions and blocking out my needs, wants, or gifts. As I changed and left the relationships, ideas, and lifestyle that no longer matched who I wanted to be, balance returned. It is still a daily spiritual practice of mine to keep myself in balance. To keep myself on track.

I began to recognize that so much of what I practiced and believed in secret was considered taboo under other names and that they were wrong. But that is also where I recognized that by labeling rituals, beliefs, practices, etc., we have destroyed ourselves. Those who were like me—who can see what I can see, do what I can do—we used to walk around like gods among the people. We would heal the sick, mend the broken, and usher in peace and presence. But we also ushered in chaos and power. We didn't have to hide who we were; I began to recognize and remember myself in those past lives. I saw resemblances in Greek mythology and how it was based on us and our giftings. I began to push the bounds of the normal, and with that, I found that there literally are no limits to what we could do. Nothing is impossible, but nothing surprises me anymore. Now, I work with dragons, fae, mermaids, mythical creatures, and the deities of old in my spiritual and healing practices on a daily basis.

During one deep metaphysical meditation, I specifically set the intention to know my past. I went back as far in my timeline as I possibly could after my witnessing of creation. I was thrust into the war of the gods. I saw before me the war between angels with "mythical" creatures that were straight out of Greek Mythology, or more like Harry Potter. Dragons, griffins, and pegasus flew through the air with other angels and deities fighting and clashing. Lightning shot like bolts through the air. Some of those beings who were able to wield the power of the Source had decided they no longer needed humanity nor "the Creator" to rule them. They had enough. They wanted to be their own gods here on earth. They all could create, so why not have all this power for themselves? Thus, a war between us broke out. The heavens flashed with power and energy, and we fought against each other. A war between those of us who would stay to serve the greater good, human choice, and the original foundation of Earth's creation, protecting the Source and committing to the human race versus those who would want to serve themselves by becoming and staying "gods" of their own power. In this war, we decimated humanity. Our war rained down from the heavens onto Earth, killing and destroying the planet we had become a part of. I personally believe this is when the dinosaurs became extinct. But this was also a pivotal moment when organized religion was born. They (humanity and darker forces) couldn't let this happen again. They needed to strip away our power. To rein us in. The power that every one of you beautiful angels of light has. And yes, even those of you fallen angels who fought against us have that power as well. But it is time for all of us to wake up, and our descendants too. And it is time to come home. We must come back to ourselves, into our power. Back into unity.

The next day, I had a friend and his wife come over for dinner. This is a beautiful couple that I have only known for a few years, but I always felt safe to share my true self with. I told them of my vision and memory that I had just received a few days prior. My male friend informed me that I was referring to stories from the *Mahabharata* and the *Bhagavad Gita*. I had never heard of those texts. So, I looked it up. It was simply confirmation that my knowing, my truth, was correct. Trust yourself, beautiful beings, even on the things that do not make sense. Because we have all the answers inside of us. We have simply forgotten or chosen to remain asleep. But you can awaken to your truth when you are ready if you are willing to do the work to get there.

I feel most religions have some sort of account of this war. Christianity specifically references it in Revelation and with the end times and the fall of Satan. It is easy to sit there and compare our beliefs, fighting, judging, and believing only one to be right over the other. But what I have found in my journey here on earth is that labels of right or wrong, true or false, have put us out of balance.

We are all different. Yet we are here for a reason. What is your reason? What is your truth? Who were you before you became that flesh and bone mass sitting on the couch reading this book?

We all can find the answers if we are willing to look. It's getting past the fear that is the hardest. Being willing to be misunderstood. Being willing to be wrong and let our truth change. It is in allowing the yin and yang to function together while being strong in **your individual truth**. What I've learned so far in my 36 years on Earth is that as scary as my truth can seem, when it comes to what other people will think of me or my beliefs, I would rather be thought of as delusional than ever go back into the dark again.

CHAPTER 5

DARK NIGHTS AND KUNDALINI AWAKENINGS

I think it is important to state once again, as I share my story, that you are reminded that your truth may be different. Take what resonates for you. Take what you feel will help you to reach the highest potential. What will help you wake your slumbering spirit? Then, as you learn even more, dive even deeper into your truth, exit the matrix, and give yourself space to change your beliefs, your views, this does not mean that the truths you held before were wrong or had no merit. In fact, quite the opposite is true. Remember the optical illusion? Your truth is a piece of art infinitely shifting and changing.

In order to have our Kundalini Awakening, as we begin to heal mentally and spiritually, we all experience what is referred to as "a Dark Night of the Soul." This is an area of your life where you not only acknowledge you cannot continue life where it is, but you decide and make the steps to let go of the patterns, thoughts, and ideas that are no longer serving you. A lot of times, this can be triggered by an event that has you "hit your rock bottom," so to speak.

But our changes and our growth don't stop with one event. We live in a world that has closed its eyes to magic. A world that has convinced us that we are not who we once were. That you do not have access to the magic, the Source, or the miracles you once performed and used every day. We are taught to be closed-minded: worshiping only with others who think exactly like you do, following a rule book based on fear and control, versus looking within and knowing yourself deeply. It takes a lot of healing to trust yourself. To not feel like you need others as a sounding board. But that is when you get to your magic. When you know that, you can know yourself deeply. When you acknowledge deep down who you are and who you are meant to be. We sometimes ignore who we once were and still are because it seems too far to be true.

In order to find who we are now, we have to be willing to embrace who we once were—and that is scary. Especially with what many call the *witch wound*. There was a time when magic and miracles were an everyday occurrence, but to most, they have become nothing but fairy tales and imaginations. But as you begin to practice your own beliefs and exercise your own strengths, you will find that you have a spiritual family waiting to help guide you back into your power. It took me over 30 years of my life before I finally began to feel safe enough to tell anyone who I knew myself to be. To talk about my knowledge of my "inhumanness." To speak on my memories. My past lives. My truths that were coming back to me.

Your dark night will begin as you remember that you are more than just human. That you are something more, even if your name wasn't written in the textbooks. You have to begin to speak about your truth, being willing to exit the matrix we live in and stand firm in. You need to be willing to let your children discover who they are at a young age, for many of you have or are giving birth to angels, old souls, and other ethereal beings who are ready to usher in this new earth. A place where the frequency of unconditional love and acceptance comes into power once again.

There is a lot of fear that will come up as you begin to own this truth. A lot of fear will begin to manifest itself, and it will take over if you let it. I think it is important to sit down and find the root of this fear. Is it what other people think of you? Religious conditioning? Is it the fear of being wrong? Imposter syndrome? Once you find the root, you can dig carefully around it, calling on your guides for help and getting the answers you seek and the healing you crave.

Even being fully secure in who I am, in my memories, in having a supportive friend group, loved ones, parents, and a community that not only supports my truth but believes it with me, I used to catch myself getting scared of abandonment and rejection. You reach a point where it doesn't matter anymore. You are at peace within yourself so deeply that the waves others might toss around no longer hurt you.

The Golden Age is returning, and your truth is too important to overlook. If, as I am speaking, you are getting an emotional response of any kind, then hear it for the battle cry of self-love that it is. Know that this book is for you. The steps are for you. Your soul self is ready to wake up and move forward into a full embrace of yourself. You are one of the slumbering gods of old, one of the sleeping beings of light, one of the fae, dragons, or more. You are one of those who can access the power of the Source directly. One of those with the means to awaken into a new state of consciousness and being. Let go of your fear, and know that I and other spiritual leaders will walk with you. But it is important you take EVERYTHING we all say and run it through your own truth. For you will never abandon you, and your higher self is bringing you to this place, this fork in the road where you can decide. Do you move forward and begin to become who you came here to become? Or do you live a life in the shadows, hiding, wishing you would have let yourself experience more?

This decision right here brings your dark night of the soul. It brings you to the path of your Kundalini Awakening.

For some, your dark night could be when you let your addiction take over your life, the loss of a loved one, or the loss of yourself or your own insight. Your dark night could be darker than others, but lighter than some. There is no comparison, for it is your journey and your journey alone. It is a time and a place where you know you have to exit the matrix. You know that you can no longer live the life of a lie that feels so misaligned deep in your soul. It is a place where you know that you must let go and go against those things that you upheld for so long.

It's seeing your own truth from a different angle and being willing to let it change, shift, and transform into something else.

A Kundalini Awakening is described by so many in different ways. Some describe it as a painful physical experience, and others as a moment where you feel as if you are losing your mind as your ego exits control and the soul essence of who you are comes to life at the driver's seat of your existence. For me, it was both physically and mentally painful. It was a time of my life when I began to put a voice to the lie I had been living. The lie of happiness, holiness, codependency, and more. But it was also where I embraced my spiritual gifts and decided that they would no longer stay in hiding. My Kundalini Awakening was fast-tracked with EMDR therapy. EMDR is a therapy designed to pull out and relive blacked-out or traumatic memories and conditioned patterns in a safe environment so you can not only face them but also rid them of their power over your subconscious decisions and reactions. I did EMDR with a therapist I trusted, along with my own deep energetic work. It was a literal rewiring of the brain with new neuro pathways. I partnered this with my own inner energy work lighting up of all my energetic chakras, as old traumas were released and new energetic flow came back into play. It hurt. It was hard. It was worth it. My future self, the now-me, thanks me immensely for taking on the temporary hardship to get to a place of absolute peace.

I asked my guides to share with you all what it is exactly,

as it is hard to put into words. **It is important to note when chan-neling any spirit, entity, ghost, etc., sometimes the correct words can be misconstrued as you are placing knowledge and wisdom from a com-pletely different dimension onto paper.** I have an entire chapter in this book of channeled texts from other deities and beings of old. It is not always easy putting the spirit onto paper, so if something doesn't make sense to you, reread it, asking your-self what it means at that moment. Each time you read it, you can gain different insights, again like the optical illusion. This is the message I received when I asked my guides about how to share with you what a Kundalini Awakening is:

For each person, their Awakening is different, yet for all, it is the same. It is where each of what you call and observe as chakras align and come to life, but even more than that, it is where the deep roots of who you are reach down into your life well. Into the source of who you are and allow you to connect directly to your-self. Your higher self. Your highest self. A Kundalini Awakening is when you join us spiritual beings and entities on another plane of existence while simultaneously existing where you are. Now, this is not to say that you were not parallel existing before because you always have existed in multiple truths and realities simultaneously, but it is to say that you stopped and took note of this shift, entering it freely with sight. You can feel the vibra-tions from other dimensions begin to reverberate through your body. You can feel the knowing, the excitement, the love of who they are inside of you. It is the embodiment of all things that were once destroyed out of fear and misunderstanding. Out of ignorance and unaligned. You do not need to know what your dark night looks like, for as you begin to pursue your journey, it will come. You do not need to look for it. But what you do need to do is go forth knowing that as you do, if you want to grow, you must be willing to shift and transform. A Kundalini Awakening is remembering yourself. It is coming home to yourself. It is no longer living the lie that has been reprogrammed into this para-digm for so long. It is a self-acceptance. A self-love.

Many of you hear these words, and they ring hollow. You feel like I have yet to give you the answers, yet the answers are already inside of you. You have but to connect to yourself to get them. You numb yourselves with drugs, alcohol, distraction, and business instead of stopping to see what it is inside of you that is ready to come online.

A Kundalini Awakening is an accepting of your truth. The truth of who you are: angel, demon, spirit, "alien," traveler, sprite, fairy, and much more importantly, a spiritual being simply having a human experience. It is where you no longer can deny your truth because your inner knowing is stronger than what you know as the ego. It is where you are fully embodying the soul in the body.

In the process of Awakening, you will feel much like an earthquake that leaves cracks in the sand of the desert, yet out of that sand, beauty arrives. Grass grows, leaves come, and water flows. You may feel at the deepest and darkest as your life breaks into a million pieces, where up is down and down is up, and nothing ever seems to make sense anymore. But as your heart centers begin to beat, as your light begins to flow, as you find yourself fully into who you are, I will be there. Your angels and guides are waiting for you on the other side to walk you through it. We are waiting to bring you to the place you once called home.

Your world is shifting; you can feel this. Some look and seek only the negatives, and even something as beautiful as a Kundalini Awakening can be viewed as deadly for some who are not willing to be transformed, shifted, broken, and remade.

You quote scriptures, religious texts, and inspirational poems, yet they ring hollow to your ears because you see the vibrations that now come behind every word others speak. That is if you allow yourselves. There are many who have begun to awaken and then realize the journey is too hard. They do not wish to continue on the path of change. Sometimes this is due to fear. Other times, this is due to unsurety. You do not know how to get to Point A from Point B. The beautiful thing about bringing balance, much like my sister Devin pointed out, is to allow yourself to flow. Let your feminine and masculine be intertwined in a way where you are both strong and powerful, divine and free. This, my friends, is your Kundalini guidebook. This is what it is like to Awaken. No one way is the right way. You must find the way that speaks to your soul. Your heart. Follow that nudging of both interest and intrigue. Know that it was put in you for a reason.

What did my dark night of the soul look like? It was being willing to walk away from abusive and toxic relationships. It was recognizing that I wasn't responsible for the healing journey of others; it was up to them to open their eyes and choose to see. It was both physically and mentally painful as I reprogrammed my mind to let go of falsehoods and beliefs that I now knew were not true. At one point, I described it to a friend as if my body was covered in a million ants. That I was being bitten over and over again. It was trembling in bed as my body leaked out 34 years' worth of black aura, blockages, trauma, and more.

I remember in the midst of my Kundalini Awakening, fully aware of what I was going through, recognizing I would never be the same, I could never step back into the codependent, self-denying people-pleasing patterns that I was once in that I had a very vivid dream. I had a hysterectomy four years prior, but this dream was so real that I knew it had meaning, and I have since seen it come to fruition.

My dream:

I was in the same setting in the dream world as I was in the 3D. I was sleeping in my bedroom, and I began to have contractions. I woke up to feeling my stomach cramp up as contraction after contraction took place. I thought to myself that this didn't make sense; I knew I was not pregnant. I had a hysterectomy; what is this? They intensified, and I felt a gush of warm liquid flow out between my legs. I jumped up and ran to the bathroom. I had blood dripping down my legs. I was in labor somehow, with something. Sitting on the toilet, the contractions became stronger and stronger. Suddenly, my mother was there watching me from the other side of the bathroom. The walls disappeared, and I was in the astral; I could see some of my guides in there waiting for me as I did what I needed to do. As the contractions intensified, I felt the need to push. I gave "birth" to this tar-like black bob. It reeked of toxicity, hatred, shame, guilt, traumas, and conditioning, not only from this life but others in the past. I had given birth to my toxicity, getting out of my essence and giving it a name. I pulled it out of this timeline where it could no longer serve me. I let it go and felt the tangible release and healing of no longer having that in my body.

Then I awoke. I was never the same again and never wanted to go back to who I was.

CHAPTER 6

RELEASING THE LABELS

When I first began to embrace my gifts, I was so scared of letting more than a few people know who I was told I was, what I believed, and what I could do. I was afraid of being seen as evil, weird, crazy, etc. Going through a divorce, I was afraid to have it used against me somehow. I was afraid of my practices being misunderstood or seen as, heaven forbid, that taboo name—witchcraft. But why do we let any label define us? It reminds me a lot of the show on Netflix: *The History of Curse Words*. Once you know where it comes from and how it has been taken and turned into something "wrong/evil," it loses its power. Some of them just make you shake your head.

But we have taken away the root of who we are and applied a label to them as good or evil. Yet, if we look back into our religious texts, we will see so many similar things were used and considered non-taboo and even holy across the board. The idea of crystals having any type of magic or healing properties may astound some, yet crystals and their healing powers date back to BC. Even the temple leaders in the Bible were given specific stones to place in their crowns, breastplates, and much more to guard the chakras. What about the incense that most religions and pagan practices alike require to be burned in order to sanctify or cleanse a space?

Labels and religious conditioning have bound us with fear. It has destroyed the deep respect of Mother Earth and the place we call home. It has taken us from viewing Earth as a gift and a place that we should revere and cherish to a portal we are just using to pass through until we get to our real home in heaven/paradise. This is a lie. We exist in multiple dimensions and realities, and sometimes, at the same time; we must release the labels and respect where we are now.

What if you take a moment and just open your mind to the possibility that you are more than "just human," that you have spiritual gifts of magic and deep energetic healing? That you chose to be here? That you may choose to come back here or be sent by the Source for another reason in the future? What if you stop for a moment and open your mind to the idea that there is a different truth than the one that you have dug your feet into the sand and refused to alter? I'm not asking you to change your beliefs if, on a deep soul level, it does not align. What I am asking is that you remember just how small Earth is in the grand scheme of the entire universe. I ask that you keep in mind how truth has changed even through the ages you are familiar with. I mean, a few centuries ago, we believed the Earth was flat. I ask that you remember that despite the fact that we like to pretend we know everything and we are determined to hold to the truth of this, time and again, we find that we were wrong. There is more to this world than your eye can see. You can taste it and feel it. You can sense and work with the magic and energetic network if you heal, come into balance, and open yourself back up to the Source. Open yourself up to the possibility that you could be wrong. You were created with the power of the Creator running through your very veins.

I was talking with a friend once about the power of the words we use. I was speaking on the consequences of labels and how we need to take back our power. She stated: "Why do you think it's called spell-ing?" I asked her to explain, and it hit me: **What we say puts into motion the energies of the universe, like casting a spell.**

The power of positive thoughts and thinking is something

that has long been studied, and not for this book. However, I do think it is very important not to ignore the fact that our words do, in fact, have power. There have been scientific studies now that show when we reminisce over a negative experience for as little as five minutes, our bodies react and create adrenaline and active proteins that have negative consequences on us for six hours! Likewise, if we stop and think of something positive and focus, a counter protein is produced that brings balance, peace, and restoration to our nervous system for eight hours. It's amazing what science can show, isn't it? The power of our thoughts and the words we speak have a visceral response in our bodies.

Before we go any further, let's dive into the history of some words and labels that I was terrified of being called as I transitioned into fully embracing myself and their true meaning. Maybe for those of you who are scared to continue or put this book in the pile of evil, it will help you hold on a little longer:

Witch: The word *witch* means *wise*. It became associated with evil as the word was changed to witchcraft, connecting it to the idea of manipulation. This transpired around the time the printing press came out.

Pagan/paganism: The original term pagan or paganism was in reference to the religions of ancient Greece, Rome, and surrounding areas. This usually had a belief in a chief god as the head of many lesser gods. But they also hold to the belief that nature is sacred and living. Not to be looked at lightly and taken for granted. That everything in nature and life can carry a profound spiritual meaning and always circle back to each other. This goes for humans, animals, plants, and so much more. Nowadays, pagan rituals and practices have a combination of religious practices, ceremonies, and beliefs blending Celtic, Greco-Roman, Native American, Norse, and Ancient Egyptian traditions.

Weird: Meant destiny. Someone who was labeled as *weird* was actually moving towards their destiny.

Taboo: This word actually came in regard to our menstrual cycles. It became something that was not meant to be talked about. Hence taboo. This disempowers women in a big way, as women are connected to Mother Earth and her magic. Every single being, human or more, on Earth must come out of the womb of a woman and only after the purity of the menstrual cycle begins and ends.

Medicine Men/Women: They used the energy of the plants and universe, understanding the natural world to find medicines given by our mother earth.

Many of the witch hunts put into play by organized religion served as a way to separate us from our truth. They burned our books. Murdered those in power and acceptance of who they were. They picked and chose what would show up in their religious texts while claiming their way was the only way. This is the only place answers exist. Then, slowly, we began to forget. The alternative to remembering and practicing our own ways was death. This is something that is deeply engrained inside of us. A past life wound of fear that needs to not only be faced but healed. I have found this is especially hard for those of us who come from a Christian or other religious background.

I was terrified of people taking my beliefs and putting me in a box with others that I felt I was far from. My intentions were pure, but I doubted myself. I think they call it *impostor syndrome*. I doubted that I could be seen as sane and loving if I was rejecting what I had been told was the only truth since I was a little girl. I was scared, but it was in giving myself the freedom to find what resonated with me, to give myself permission to seek my own truth, my own beliefs, my own religious, or lack of, values that I found deep inner healing, access to all the magic I felt I had lost and reconnected myself to my soul essence.

As you begin to explore your power, find yourself again. Know that it is your intention behind your practices that matters. There are many people who can do what I do energetically but pull from the dark side. Their intentions are self-seeking, self-serving, and always looking for ways to lift themselves up, even to the detriment of others. Sometimes, they are taught this way generationally, with beliefs and practices passed down from one generation to another, and other times, they learn through other sources and love how it makes them feel. And sometimes it is because of who they, or you, are. But we can all come back into our power and regain our understanding in peace and love. Again, it is about the intention you put behind it.

 # CHAPTER 7 

WAKING UP

I won't pretend that being awake in a sleeping world is easy. There are moments when I hear myself speak my truth and it seems to echo into silence. I used to shake my head and judge those who sounded just like me. Before my Awakening, in a misguided attempt to find myself and help others do so too, I had pushed organized religion, the church, Jesus, and black-or-white lifestyles onto others. Trusting ourselves is something that we have been trained for so long to never do. It has been ingrained in us to follow under an umbrella of societal thinking, religious living, and gatekeeping choices that have kept us from fully knowing ourselves. Knowing ourselves is something many of us have forgotten how to do.

One of the most amazing things I ever did for myself was allow my inner goddess, the inner angel, to rule my life. I am able to reach out in unconditional love to all those who hurt me both intentionally and unintentionally and let go through spiritual soul ties, practices, and rituals. What I find amazing is the more I embraced myself and the knowing that was inside of me, the more I remembered. The more my higher self came back to being.

I not only remember creation being formed, but I remember walking the Earth with other angelic brothers and sisters taking on the names of old: Athena, Ishtar, Aphrodite, Medusa, Krishna, so many names labeled by so many religions, yet they were simply spiritual beings fully able to embrace themselves during their human experience as I am learning to do now, as YOU are learning to do. We once walked the Earth together as gods, healing humanity and loving them into higher vibrations while immersing ourselves in their human experience and culture. I remember being on other planets and in other dimensions. Many times, as you hone your giftings, you can actually layer these realities on top of each other, seeing two or more at once.

This life, this beautiful, pure spiritual way of being, is the only way for me to live now. Maybe for you, it is the way that has been calling out to you from of old, trying to get you to come home. If you've felt the tug, if you have felt the calling, it is because you are not merely human. There is something so much deeper to you. You have just forgotten. You have access to magic once again: manifestation, astral projection, energetic, spiritual and physical healings, bottomless wealth, dream-making, and so much more.

Your time is now to remember who we are. We are beings created of pure love by the hands of the Mother. Beings made of pure light by the Source. We are all connected by energetic networks that know no time, space, or prison. Energy is all, and all is energy. If you think this is speaking in riddles, it is only because you have yet to take the blinders off your eyes. You have yet to silence the noise and think for yourself. Stop believing your truth and purpose is only what everyone else tells you that it is.

Let's think of it this way. If, as a kid, you are shown the color blue, and your entire life, you are taught that it is actually called yellow. You are ingrained with this truth so heavily that you cannot believe someone when they share the real truth with you. You have believed all your life that blue was called yellow. But when you open your mind to the thought that there is more than one truth. That yellow, in fact, is a part of blue only added in things that have been missing your whole life.

Deep down, you know who you are. Your higher self, the being, and the spirit you were before coming into this body, is there waiting for you to stop the karmic circle of self-punishment, break those generational chains of curses and trauma, and bring from it the inner generational wisdom of lifetimes in knowing how to find yourself and where to bring your healing to. You are beautifully and wonderfully made. A beautiful creature from the Source.

We have to stop pretending that we already have all the answers. I have said it time and again: I am not here to convince you of your own truth. But I am here to share mine. Maybe in doing so, it will allow you to find yours.

CHAPTER 8

LETTING GO AND EGO DEATH

One important thing to note is how hard it is to let go. To let go of the idea of how you should have lived. To let go of how you have been expected to live. This isn't saying that your spiritual awakening allows you to break the rules and live a life on the edge with no regard for how anyone else is affected in the name of being true to oneself. In fact, true spiritual awakenings where you are fully embracing yourself are going to naturally cause you to give back to others in your actions, thoughts, deeds, and vibrations.

You live a life that may make some uncomfortable. Others are inspired, and others are wary, but they are all still watching. Jesus, Mohammed, and the Buddha all made people very uncomfortable. We naturally do not like change.

Letting go of your ego and allowing it to no longer be the thing that controls you is known as an *ego death*. It is the peeling away of preconditioned patterns, self-destructive thoughts, and societal expectations and getting to the base of who you are. You at the very root. Some of you, as you go through your Kundalini Awakening, will have quantum leaps in your healing where you will move so fast that people will begin to question if you are bipolar or having a nervous breakdown. You yourself may have thoughts like, What am I doing? This is opposite to what I would normally choose, and so this is scary, but in the end, you feel that deep, deep tug that there is no other way.

When I died to myself, my ego, and I let myself reawaken, it was one of the scariest things I had to do. Even writing this book, knowing that I was coming from a Christian background, that some who once called me a friend or acquaintance may read it, at first, gave me pause. But the more I became grounded in self-love and self-acceptance, the less their opinions of me mattered. I knew I had no other choice but to be authentically me from now on. Some would argue that point, saying there is always a choice. But the truth of the matter is, when you finally feel free to be yourself in the deepest essence of the miracle of who you really are, then there is no one else that you can be. The choice is made for you, but it doesn't take that fear away.

If you are someone like I was in the past, I would hear people talk of astral projection, parallel timelines, Egyptian deities, and Akashic Records and think they were absolutely mad bonkers. But things always look muggy when you are wearing the dirty glasses of conditioning over your eyes. It is about taking off what others put on there, what you put on there, what you feel is required, and allowing yourself the freedom to really know who you are.

When I finally let go, I was triggered into a massive episode of PTSD accompanied by "fight or flight." I knew I wanted to leave my husband, my church, my at-the-time core beliefs I had tried to uphold all my life. I knew in doing this, I was also going to lose a lot of friends. It physically hurt to rewire my brain and let new neuro-pathways form and take me to a place of safety. In fact, I worked very closely with the help of a trained professional doing EMDR and monitoring my mental state before moving forward on big decisions to be sure that I was thinking clearly.

Once I reached a place of safety, a place where I wasn't constantly surrounded by the noise of everyone telling me I had to be a certain way, or even myself for that matter, I was able to surrender to who I already knew I was. Who I was done hiding as. I was able to explore my truth, my spiritual gifts, and all that came with that.

Letting go will be scary. Imposter syndrome may kick in, telling you that you are not special. That you are making up the changes, the visions, the dreams. That you are not normal. Guess what? That is exactly right. You are not normal. You are what I like to refer to as a "majestic neurodivergent spiritual being." You are created more than human. More than this human experience made you believe. But you also came down for such a time as this. You came down to know yourself, to be yourself, to heal your past and present lives. It is time to move forward step by step.

CHAPTER 9

STEPS TO FINDING YOUR TRUTH

When you embrace YOUR truth, not the truth you have been conditioned to believe, not the lies you have been told in where your identity lies, but the true truth, then you find freedom. How is this? Where does it start? It starts with love.

Love for yourself. Self-love *in life*, not just in a moment. Speaking kindly to yourself and reparenting yourself to the space of who you were before you came face to face with hardships in the physical world. It is deconditioning yourself to the trauma of who you have become. It is letting go of the need to explain or rationalize. It is finding your joy and living in that high vibration every day.

One of the things I had to do in order to find my healing was to look at my life and stop diminishing those things that were hard. I had to stop diminishing the abuse I endured over the years, both from myself and others. I had to recognize and name the things that made me feel worthless, useless, and call them for the lies that they were. I had to face those things for how they truly made me feel and then get to the why. I had to let myself feel it all.

In this day and age, we are so set on pressing forward. Being a conqueror and overcomer. We idolize people who can make us say, *They put everyone first above themselves.* But what kind of life did they have then? Were they meeting their own needs? Are you getting your needs met? Some of you can say *yes* and be truthful. But I think the majority of us are stuck in the same pattern I was in. Stuck in a place of believing that the only way to move forward would be by denying a lot, if not all, of ourselves and giving to others. Allowing ourselves to only embrace the parts of our truth found in the mainstream belief systems and knowledge. It may feel like you have to have external validation in order to have your words have value or meaning.

Where do we go from here? For starters, you must be willing to go against the grain. Go against the space in which humanity would have you be currently. Set yourself up for success with a few supporters or the mental health support you may need as you begin to face the fear. Know that even as relationships walk away from you when you decide to wake up, others will come in their stead eventually, as you grieve what you lost. As they do, that pain will not be so hard or unbearable.

What is your truth? Guess what the magical part of this is? You get to discover it! You get to find out what it is on your own! And that is half the fun once you reach a place of safety to explore.

How does one discover their truth? How does one wake up in a sleeping world? Where do we even start? The first key is to not deny that little inkling of curiosity in the back of your mind. It is there for a reason. There is a reason that you are feeling curious about natural medicine, folklore, Greek mythology, meditations, etc.; our curiosity speaks to us. Many people coming from religious organizations or fundamentalist backgrounds immediately condemn what is not understood. Stop and look for a moment at the *why*. Why would this be condemned? It is condemned because it is misunderstood.

You must get to know yourself. There are a lot of people who feel fully that their opinions and thoughts are their own, but if you were to look deep enough, you would discover it is a parroting of what you were taught in childhood, conditioned with patterns and beliefs that keep you trapped in a place where you are *happyish*. But what if I told you that by opening your mind to the possibility that your opinion could change if you gained more information? What if it didn't want to change after? How much sweeter would your beliefs be?

We must stop the comparison game. The thought that we know it all and are so much better than this person because this person is living a lifestyle we don't agree with. We are in a huge awakening phase, where love of others is becoming something we are reaching out towards, but the problem is, there are a lot of us who will love others to our own detriment. It is time to start loving yourself and treating yourself with the same respect and boundaries that you do for others.

You find your truth by knowing yourself. By spending time alone, quietly, going back to your childhood hardships and traumas while not minimizing what you went through. We know ourselves by allowing ourselves to feel the emotions we have trapped and stored in our bodies. We know ourselves by getting to the root soul of who we were, back before we came into this human form. We find our truth by embracing our soul in our body with our mind. No longer ignoring and betraying the self.

How? I feel like many of you are saying: You say this and make it sound so easy, but I know I have trauma; I know I have triggers. What now? You do the work required to live the way you want to live. To live in the moment, unreactive. When you find yourself ruminating (thinking back and reliving negative experiences from the past), you call yourself on it and say: *"I'm ruminating; this is no longer helpful for me in my life and serves no purpose in helping me heal, so I am releasing it and coming back to the present."*

Some easy steps to follow as you begin to awaken:

Begin to journal your feelings in the moment: Right now, I feel x, y, z, but then follow that thread. Why? Why do you feel that way? You will begin to step out of your reactive mind, giving space for your spiritual soul to take over and your higher self to guide you.

Begin to meditate: Meditation is a conscious act where we put our body and mind aside and allow our soul to come into the space of pure and whole consciousness. It is a place where you pour into yourself. Start with just five minutes of quiet reflection. Put on some music, find a guided app—there are many options—and begin to learn to be still even in the chaos of your own mind. Too many people think meditation is about thinking of nothing. I was one of them. I would say I can't meditate because I can't stop thoughts in my mind. But it is quite the opposite. Meditation is about sitting back and observing the fact that you are indeed a soul in the human body. You allow yourself to separate the three: body, soul, and mind. You allow the soul to sit back and observe the mind as it ping-pongs from thought to thought like an echo in a cave. But you don't follow the thoughts down the rabbit hole. You stop and begin to focus on your breathing if you notice yourself having difficulty. Think of it like connecting the dots: breathe in, breathe out, with an even flow of a figure-eight, never stopping. Eventually, you learn to put those thoughts to the side and sit in nothingness. Then, as you get even deeper, you come to the veil of consciousness.

Meditative growth happens in three stages:

Stage One: You have thoughts that ping-pong, and you must learn to let them simply come and go.

Stage Two: You begin to get pictures and visions in your mind, much like a movie.

Stage Three: You come to the veil exiting the 3D. You get so deep into letting your soul just be in your body, ignoring the rants of the mind and images, that you cross what I like to describe as a hidden veil. You feel it, you can tell it is there, and you choose to actively step past it into complete peace. Into the astral. It is in this space where you can manifest magic into your life. You can call in healing, blessings, love, abundance, peace, and so much more. It is from here that you can set the intentions to visit Akashic records, past lives, visit with spirit guides, etc. And it is then that you will see visions come to your mind, much like a movie, only you can converse, talk, and gain full awareness and understanding of who you are and other beings.

I feel like I could write an entire book by itself on meditation, but I also do not feel that is my purpose. My purpose here is to help you awaken. To orchestrate your Kundalini Awakening. To allow you to embrace the inner power you have known is there all along but that you have been scared to claim. Let us not run in fear from those things that are different; instead, let's face why they scare us. You'll find they aren't so scary after all.

CHAPTER 10

ACCEPTING YOUR TRUTH:
A CHANNELED MESSAGE FROM THE GUIDES

For this chapter what is written will be a mixture of channeled messages from some of my guides, deities of old, and spiritual beings in general. I will let you know when each is speaking. Some of you will feel energetic pulls as certain ones are channeled into this book, like a magnet pulling at your soul. Pay attention to that, as you most likely are one of them, energetically linked to them in some way, or have more to learn about them. As stated above, channeled messages are done in a way that translates a ninth-dimensional or higher language frequency down to 3D words; it is my best interpretation of what they say. Know you can read their messages over and over again and gain different perspectives, but all should be filtered through yourself to see if they resonate.

I do know that accepting your truth can seem like one of the scariest things you can ever do when you are coming from a place of conditioned thinking. I know there are several groups that, in general, are more open to the idea that we are more than we seem, but overall, there is a collective fear that seems to arise as we try to fit in a box, so to speak. We are afraid to be too out there because maybe then we will not be able to come back from what we say, maybe we won't be taken seriously, maybe we will be made to feel inferior. A big part of knowing yourself is knowing that your thoughts, even if they differ from others, are important. They are needed. You are needed. It is knowing and giving yourself permission to not only change, but to continue to evolve. Look at your change as healing versus hypocritical. You came here, beautiful soul, to raise the vibration of Earth. Don't be so afraid of getting it wrong that you don't give yourself permission to truly get it right.

Now it is time for Channeled Messages from the following:

Gaia

Athena

Isis

Pleiadean Star Mother

Arcturian Queen

Dragons: Blue, Black, and White

Fairy Goddess

Goddess Izzabell

GAIA

For years, you have been taught how to forsake my ways. How to ignore the land, the fruits, and the plants that give life. Instead, looking at me, at them, like an inconvenience that must be harnessed. You sought out perfection from things that were already perfect, even in the imperfections.

My children sing songs to me on the wind; you look at them as pests that must go. They dance and frolic in the field, and you look at them like meat for your dinner tables. There is the circle of life; of that, I am not naive, for even my children partake in their own circles, but they do it in a way that is natural and homely. Nothing going to waste, all feeding the land of which they came, they do it in a way that brings love and life and laughter to their breed of families and others. You do not need to stop all that you are doing, but simply stop what is no longer serving you.

Stop and listen to my words in the winds. Stop and listen to the songs that I give you. Remove yourself from the constant chaos that is there in the mornings from the moment that you wake up. Give yourself the freedom to explore, to know me for yourself, not who you have been taught to believe is there. I am all around you, even those of you who live in the cities, for even you cannot escape my winged and long-tailed children, the blue skies, or rainy days. I am everywhere all at once. I am there all at once. You have but to bring mutual respect to the land, such as asking a flower for permission before cutting or asking it to remove its energy first, recognizing that even the trees are teaming with life and abundance; they have souls and families. It is a matter of knowing that I am with you in every place that you tread.

You want to know how to get back to your roots? Find a way to escape the distractions that you always put on yourself. You make yourself so busy so that you do not have time to sit with me, but rather, it is not that you do not have time; you have other priorities. I am not here to say do this, eat this, drink this. I am to tell you to come back to me knowing that my roots, my spirit, are still in the deep debts of the earth. Though some of my love has been depleted and garnished from the soil, the rocks, and the trees, just like a root system, my love runs ever deep. I have a heartbeat; the Earth beats to it.

For those of you who have an affinity for me and for those of you who would like to know me, I am ready to meet you where you are. You have but to quiet your mind, silence the noise, and ask for an audience. I will speak to you through the whisper of thoughts, of ideas through the wind, and through the trees. I will speak to you through the visions and dreams.

Those of you truly ready, I will come in tangibly to see.

Find your peace, embrace your love, and know that I am, in fact, with you in every single thing that I do. You do not have to be afraid. For those of you who have lost your empathy for my children completely, I am here to say it is never too late to re-sensitize yourself. Give yourself permission to break through the wall of all those things that have left you wanting more, forgetting that every living thing, from the grass to the animals, has a soul. All of it. Do not turn a blind eye to what is taking place, even on a small scale.

STAR MOTHER & GODDESS ISIS

This one is for the collective children who have waited lifetimes to come back to the light. Some of you have made decisions based in darkness, causing your souls to hurt and be crushed in this time. I am here to give you the strength to step back into the light, not even for yourself but for the collective of peace across the galaxies. You are a spiritual being, interdimensional, that has become trapped in this idea that this dense 3D reality is who you are. I am here to remind you that you are indeed so much more. As you read these words, know that they are coded with light language and Source. Know that they are coded to awaken you; stop for a moment with me and breathe in and out and receive:

Breathe in ... Breathe out (repeat this for several minutes like a figure-eight, never stopping but gently flowing on the breathing in and out).

As you breathe in, allow your focus to come to your heart space; even as you read this, allow my voice to ring in your mind. Allow yourself to remember that you are, in fact, a child of the stars. It is time to wake up, little ones. It is time for you to remember who you are, but not only remember but step into the power that comes with that. Do not doubt yourself as your truth comes. Wake up, little ones, and remember that you are a son or daughter of Zeus; you are kings and queens in your own right. Step into your power; step into who you are and who you know yourself to be. Love yourself on the way. Love yourself in all things you are seeing, and love yourself where you know you have been imperfect. For we do make mistakes despite what we are, but put your intention into growth, into self-knowing, self-love, self-movements, and self-expression, and do it all in love, for love is, in fact, the highest of all vibrations. As you learn to forgive yourself, heal your wounds, and dive deeply into who you are meant to be. Watch yourself transform into something incredible. You, my child, are special, always. You have always been. You are about to have your giftings unlocked and know who you are.

Rest as you need to rest; do not try to do it all at once. Know that you are being guided by my light and the light of love with many other guides. Take things one step at a time and rest in love.

ATHENA

Many of you know me, but you know me by a false version told in your fairy tales. I am a protector of Source, of humanity, wanting to fight to get our power back, but in a way that brings us back into harmony, not destruction. I am fully integrated into the universes, the earths, and the waters. I fight alongside all the gods of old to defeat those things that feed on chaos and destruction.

Many of you have lost your fight. You have lost who you know yourself to be. You have lost what it is that you are at the very center of your source; you have lost where you are meant to be. You play the victim and blame instead of looking at life while strategically knowing that you have full control of all things that come around you. You are the creator of all that comes your way; step by step, you sit there, and you move in a way that would be where you need not take any responsibility. But I am here to tell you there is so much power in responsibility, in taking on what it is you know you are meant to and moving forward in that way. It is not easy to achieve at first, for we are taught at a young age through life lessons that others are responsible for us. Religions teach the umbrella effect of safe authority or proper beliefs that are forcing you to stay in the midst of a cage and hold you back not only from your power but also your truth. It is time, my friends, to look to your dreams and what they are telling you. What are they speaking?

I meet with many of you there in your dream state, but you wake, and you forget how to take back your power. Begin to silence your heart and your soul and begin to pour into yourself as much as you pour into others. Begin to acknowledge that every answer that you seek is already in you. Do not stress or worry about what is to come or how it is to come; sit, quiet the noise, and let it come to you. There are many of us who sit and mentor you in dreams, but it seems a pattern that if you do not like what it is we are sharing, you seem to wipe it off your mind the moment you wake. But the thing is, all the answers you seek come between worlds as you rest. You want to know how to take back your power? Stop playing the victim; start focusing instead on what it is that you want and then on how you can realistically get it. It is time to take your power back from others that you have so freely given. In that world of social media you all seem so obsessed with, you strive for external validation instead of truth and building and edifying others. I am here to tell you that is not the way that it should be. You should be fully immersing yourself in who and where you are, knowing full well that you, YOU, have all the power and all the answers you need within yourself at all times.

How do you find your truth? How do you find your memories of old? You must first embrace warrior energy, that of your inner warrior, and say, "No more!" No more to others telling me who I am, what value I have, where I come from, and where I am going. No more to the inner truths and wisdoms coming only from this sector of energy and none other, no more allowing others to tell me what is real and what is not, and no more others telling me that I must serve them to my own detriment. It is time to wake up, sleeping children. Wake up and remember that you are gods yourselves. You are forged of the very source of the Creator here for an experience to bring you to this exact awakening. You are here to know yourself and set not only yourself free, but everyone else coming your way. You are here to alter this destructive course that humanity is on and to know yourself more and in a deeper way through remembrance, breaking the fog and setting yourself free. It is time to wake up, beautiful children, and remember who you are.

PLEIADEAN STAR MOTHER

Oh, my child, how I have longed for so long for you to awaken and allow me to speak to you in this way. You have listened for me, cried out for me, and even gotten to a point where you began to doubt yourself, for our vibrations were not at a match yet to be heard. We have never left and have always looked on and sent beams of love, light, and even help in the guise of angels, signs, and synchronicities.

You have known you are different for quite some time. You have known that you are here but don't quite fit in with the group that is there or why they are there. You may ask yourself with a shake of your head why things cannot just be simple. It is simple to love, and it is simple to be kind, but that is because you, at the root of all things, are, in fact, love, the highest of vibrations. I am here to tell you that as you continue on this journey to discover those of you whom this message is meant for, those who come from a place of Pleiadean lines or the lines of all Star Mothers will begin to feel your skin tingle at this moment, you may feel similar to goosebumps. Now, I want you to close your eyes for a few breaths and imagine a doorway opening up before you as we pour out light into you, as we activate those vibrations that are ready and meant to come. As we move you into who you are at a soul level.

You will have many moments when you feel like you have done enough, like you can let things be, but I tell you that you chose to come down to earth to usher in the golden age once more, to allow not only our light to shine but the light of the old gods once again. The fairies, druids, dragons, and gods of old. The aliens, or starseeds, as you like to call them, are all here waiting for Earth to meet the optimal time for self-love and inner harmony. While it may seem to you that things are getting so much worse, that is but a perception put on by those who would like you to stay in darkness. Think of a peacock when he spreads his beautiful tail in order to intimidate those and try to hide what is really behind him. That is how things are playing out now as the focus is given to these dark energies. It is time for you to move your focus into you, into where you want to be, who you want it to be with, and why. Do not allow anyone to have so much power over you that it takes away your peace. Your past hurts and pains, as deeply as they cut, you get to be the healer now; you get to be the generation breaker, the love balm that goes into these wounds.

Give yourself the energy of the mother, the father, the grandparents, the lover, the child. Let yourself be all things at once and allow yourself to move forward in these things. Allow yourself to rediscover your childhood; the dreams you held then have meaning. Some of you pictured going to space because you wanted to be back in the stars from which you came. Some of you wanted to train dragons because that is where you once were; some of you were obsessed with fairy tales and rescuers because you longed to get back to that place of inner harmony, while others were looking for the idea of a rescuer. I see it all, my child; we see it. We are here to impart our love, our deep healing, and our passion to you. Know that we are there with you and that we see you deeply to the very depths of your soul, to the very depths of who you are. We are here to guide you home. We will meet with you in your dreams, in your codes, in the synchronicities that seem to come every day. Just know that you are never alone; your highest self, already completed on this journey, stands with us as we walk you through to your place of triumphant healing. A place where you can come out even stronger than you once were.

Do not be afraid as you begin to awaken when you realize that you can no longer live the life you were once living, for it is in the letting go that everything else is gained. Hold on to the idea of who you are and what you want, and do not compromise for less. We are, in fact, watching you heal on a molecular level so that you are awakening your crystalline body and coming home. We are always ready to meet with you in the quiet space and recesses of your mind as you sit back and trust yourself. Now that is the key, trusting yourself, for many of you have been taught that there is but one way to live and only one, but by letting go and allowing those other things to come into you, you are, in fact, welcoming them home to you yourself. Do not be afraid; we will say it again: do not be afraid, for you are not alone. And an entire army of angels waits in the heavens to guide you on this path. Take it daily, live in the very present moment, being very true to yourself the day of, and then watch your lives transform accordingly. We love you, my sons and daughters.

ARCTURIAN QUEEN

I have been known by many names over the centuries, but the most important name you know me by is Mother. Do not allow the stars to unalign you in such a way. You all focus so much on the energy shifts and the cosmos, and while there are answers in all of those, there is also freedom. It is not meant to be a massively draining situation, but rather one of enjoyment, deep inner love, and freedom. You are meant to dance with the equinox, the solar flares, and the freedom that comes to set yourself free in all the ways as it comes. Allow your body to have what it needs: when you feel the need to change your diet, the need to change your friends, and even in so as much as changing your clothing, there is a reason: you are shifting and changing with the winds. Know that I am with you everywhere you look in the stars. My beautiful children, do not doubt yourselves or your visions; just know that you are indeed exactly where you must be. Reset yourself in the evening, look up into the stars, and allow the downloads of light from the twinkling beauties to come to you. Do not feel there is only one way for healing, for healing is infinite and always will be. Find what speaks to you in the moment you need it spoken, and you will find all the answers that you seek.

DRAGONS: BLUE, BLACK, & WHITE

Many of you have looked at us as figments of the imagination; we watch sometimes as you portray us as beasts of old. While we are old, we are also new. We still give new life to our young, we nurture the relationships between humans, and some of us are even walking around you in that human skin, confined as ever, in an effort to allow our vibrations to come back to the planet. Do not doubt or disbelieve even as you read this, for some of you are us in sleeping form, and right now, you feel that rumbling in your chest and the tears forming in your eyes. It is you that are, in fact, one of us, part of us, with us in all things. We are always ready to do battle with you, bring light to you, explore with you, and help you regain your magic. We are not dark nor evil, though some of us through time picked the dark side to stand when the war between gods broke out, but now we are back, we are here, and we collectively want nothing more than to bring you all home, for the loss of magic not only affected us but every living thing. We want to once again soar in the minds of the children like days of old. Know that we walk with you, we watch with you. If ever you need a little bit of healing, call on us and our breath and watch us begin to wake from our slumber, even if only in your mind's eye. We are always willing and able to jump out and into where you need us. We are ready to stand with you once again.

FAIRY GODDESS

My dear, beautiful children, there are many of you here on Earth, trapped in this endless cycle of self-abuse and misery. You choose not to embrace fully who you are for fear that you will be ridiculed. You see us, and you connect with us on the regular. Likewise, we pour out our love and our light to you; we pour out our insight and our help into you. Do not question your magic. It is built into the very grains of who you are. Do not doubt the reasons you live the way you live, for you have been called to forge ahead and move into the planets to bring back our glory, our energy, our vibration. Many of you, as you volunteered to come down, thought it would be much easier. You got lost along the way, but that is only because you are looking for answers externally; it is time to stop and focus on the self, on the answers that are all on the inside of you. On the answers that are with you in all that you need. Stop feeling like it needs to fit in a box. Move forward and move upward, and know that I am with you and guiding you every step of the way.

Our realm is one of magic and deep connection to the

source of all things; we are deeply rooted with Gaia and work with her and her children daily. For those of you who feel an affinity with us, you tend to find magic in everyday things. You see the beauty in the things full even of destruction. You fear being ridiculed as in the past you were imprisoned and tortured, your magical rights stripped from you and used for others. But today, we are coming together with this collective, all our vibrations forming as one gigantic wave of light and moving into what we are supposed to do: ushering in the golden age, the age of magic once more.

Look for us in the forest, in the sky, in the plants, look for us in the deep states of mediation, ask for permission, and we will meet with you, we will work with you and help you rediscover play with the energies that you once held dear. Yes, things can get a little sticky as you rediscover working with time and energetic shifts, but like riding a bike, as you continue to adjust your vibration and frequencies back home, it will come to you easily. We await your return eagerly.

GODDESS IZZABELL

Here we are, my children. Many of you come from my Pleiadian star line, but you forget because you put this idea that your circle must fall in this line and only this line. Feel me now as I break the mold. As I move forward, take you into my arms, and remind you of just how great you are. While the trials you face here on this planet seem big, they are but distractions from the game you came to play. The game where you get to experience every emotion, every experience: fear, excitement, love, hatred, all of it. But all of it is with the purpose of bringing yourself back home in the end. Do not worry about karma coming after you, for we are all children of the light, even those who had turned at one point into the dark. Move forward, following the rising and falling of the tides of inner peace. Remove the distractions that would cause you to focus on the external circumstances, and know that I am with you now every step of the way, as are your other guides and everyone else coming your way. Know that I am with you now in all things and that we, your soul family, come to bring only peace, light, and love. Once you fully embrace the light, you realize that truly nothing else can hurt you, not even in the slightest, for it all works out for the better. Keep your eyes on your heavenly body, knowing that your highest self is the one who has come out to seek you, to be with you, and to live, laugh, and love.

Enjoy the journey, but ask for help when you need it. Don't feel blind. Know that we always speak to you, on the winds, in the stars, through "coincidences," of which there truly is no such thing. We are indeed with you now every step of the way. Always.

CHAPTER 11

KUNDALANI RISING

I know firsthand how hard it is to change your beliefs, break conditioning patterns, let go of the expectations of others, and begin to live authentically in your own truth. I know how much information is out there from other leaders, guides, and people telling their opinions and truths that make it hard to distinguish up from down. I know how hard it is to step into your truth, to set boundaries, to allow yourself to "come online." I know firsthand how hard it is to accept the changes in your mind and even your body as you awaken. It is a literal rewiring of the brain, a reprogramming of the body; it is a coming alive of your crystalline light body. A simple summary of this is where your entire vibration is changing. Think of it as an actual change to your DNA where your 9D vibration is coming down to meet your 3D self and mesh in the middle. It is a rewiring of the soul, allowing yourself to come into peace and safety. It can physically hurt, it can emotionally hurt, and it can be exhausting. This doesn't mean it is not worth it or that it has to be overwhelming, for your highest self never gives you more than it knows you could do in this lifetime. This is how we can move into freedom and into peace. This is what we go through in order to let go of ourselves.

One thing I found to be false that I believed when I first started my mentor journey was the idea that we all must be aggressive in our approach to healing as we pull out all things that are not aligned, when in fact, a much gentler approach is shining a light onto what your soul knows it is ready to let go of. Let your soul come into control, and as you shine the light of the Source, something we all have access to, the energy of your soul body, the essence of who you are made of. By doing this, we are able to clean ourselves out in a much gentler (though slower approach) a lot like a stream that takes away the leaves, debris, and trash that is loose and ready to be swept away.

Personally, I know I was so focused on just wanting to be done I chose to pull out, detangle, and reset myself as fast as possible. I used my own access to Source through energetic healing to purge and cleanse myself as fast as possible. I had lived so long in the dark that I was ready to be fully in the light all the time. I wanted to be home to myself, in my soul essence. But it is not quite that simple for everyone; you need to let yourself have time to grow and heal. You need to get yourself to a place of safety physically, emotionally, and mentally, where you are *allowed* to change and grow. In time, you can let go of things as they come when the time is right. You should find a community with others who will build you up and are also committed to growth and healing.

That is why I created the program **Kundalini Rising**. As you are going through this journey, you will have moments when you NEED mental health support, community, energetic support, or sometimes just a safe space to share your experiences. Not only do I invite you to come and connect with us, but I encourage anyone in this journey of breaking habits to be raw and fully open about how you feel and allow your soul family of support to come your way. If that doesn't feel like an option, seek out mental health support that can guide you on this mission. Healing isn't something we are meant to walk alone, and though our spiritual self, guides, and family are always walking with us, when you have a physical family to walk with you, that is something that is really beyond compare.

Kundalani Rising is a step-by-step mentorship program to help you break conditioned patterns along with 12 guided energetic healing activations and monthly focuses as you come online, and embrace who you are. It is an energetic guidebook for opening your chakras and activating your full Kundalini Awakening. It is a path to access your spiritual gifts and gain back your memories of who you once were and still are. It is for those of you who feel like you need extra spiritual or energetic healing, help, and release. It is a place to get connected to open-minded and spiritually awakened mental health professionals who have partnered with me and my program to bring you to a place of safety and remembrance of who you once were and still are.

I also have my **Quantum Circle**. This allows you to gain a Weekly Collective Tarot reading and energy update. Every month we have a monthly energy update, and a monthly guided energetic activated healing session to help you prepare for the month ahead and learn, like our Arcturian Queen said, to dance with the energies. Details on all programs can be found below.

It has been an honor facilitating this book and this Awakening for you. I would love to hear your story. You may connect with me and my program in several ways:

TikTok and Instagram: **totheawakenedsouls**

Podcast (available on most platforms): **To The Awakened Soul's Podcast** by Devin Browne

Kundalani Rising Programs: **Patreon.com/kundalanirising**

You may also connect with me and our like-minded community on Facebook.

Remember, dear ones, all the answers you are seeking are already on the inside of you. Healing isn't meant nor promised to be easy, but it is promised to be worth it.

With Love,
Devin Browne
Your Kundalini Activator and Starseed

Acknowledgments

I would like to take the time to thank those who supported me through my transformation.

My Readers: Thank you for taking the time to read this letter. I hope that you found what you need to start your transformation process. Without you, this book would be nothing.

Safaa: Thank you for accepting me from the moment I spoke my truth to you. Thank you for always encouraging me to trust myself. Thank you for challenging me to grow even more into who I know I can be and who I want to become. Thank you for helping me rise above and encouraging me to show love within the midst of all my situations. Thank you for modeling to me what unconditional love looks like, and teaching me how to give that to myself. احبك دائماً.

Andie: Thank you for coming into my life as my soul family. Thank you for not only giving me the space and permission to change and transform within the relationship, but also growing with me on your own journey. I am so grateful to have you walking this beautiful path with me. I love watching you grow and transform in your own walk. Grateful to call you family.

Rebecca: Thank you for always listening to my crazy, "you won't believe this" experiences. Thank you for always keeping an open mind but also calling me on my shit. Thank you for connecting me to so many like-minded souls. Thank you for allowing me space to be me and loving me in all phases of my growth.

My Therapist: Thank you for helping me break past my conditioning patterns. Thank you for your openness and willingness to work with my circumstances, beliefs, and situations as they changed. Thank you for helping me know that it was okay to change. Thank you for walking with me backward into the deepest recesses of my mind and standing with me while I broke myself free. I am forever grateful to you.

Atmosphere Press: Thank you to my entire editing team for helping me bring this book to life. Thank you for letting me speak as openly as I needed and encouraging me along the way.

About Atmosphere Press

Founded in 2015, Atmosphere Press was built on the principles of Honesty, Transparency, Professionalism, Kindness, and Making Your Book Awesome. As an ethical and author-friendly hybrid press, we stay true to that founding mission today.

If you're a reader, enter our giveaway for a free book here:

SCAN TO ENTER
BOOK GIVEAWAY

If you're a writer, submit your manuscript for consideration here:

SCAN TO SUBMIT
MANUSCRIPT

And always feel free to visit Atmosphere Press and our authors online at atmospherepress.com. See you there soon!

About the Author

Devin Browne is an empathic energetic healer and spiritual guide. She is passionate about the growth and healing of others. Through her own experiences, spiritual connections, and journey, she hopes to help you not only find your voice, and spiritual giftings but also your truth.

www.ingramcontent.com/pod-product-compliance
Lightning Source LLC
Chambersburg PA
CBHW020746160726
47993CB00006B/2630